A Chill in the Air

Howard J. Kogan

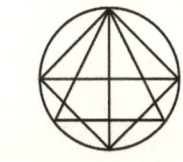

Square Circle Press
Schenectady, New York

A Chill in the Air

Published by
Square Circle Press LLC
PO Box 913
Schenectady, New York 12301
www.SquareCirclePress.com

©2016, Howard J. Kogan.
All rights reserved. No part of this publication may be reproduced or transmitted in any form or by any means, electronic or mechanical, including photocopying, recording, taping, or any other information retrieval system, without permission in writing from the publisher.

First paperback edition, 2016.
Printed in the United States of America on acid-free, durable paper.
ISBN-13: 978-0-9856926-9-8
ISBN-10: 0-9856926-9-3
Library of Congress Control Number: 2016956553

Publisher's Acknowledgments
Cover design by Richard Vang, Square Circle Press. Cover image photograph courtesy of Richard Vang.

Some of the poems in this book first appeared, in somewhat different versions as follows: "A Close Family," "Tanta Chava" and "Homers" in *Naugatuck River Review*; "First Responders" and "In the End" in the *Jewish Currents'* publications *Union* and *Urge*; "Where the Dead Live" in *Literary Gazette*; "Last Act" in *Two*; "An Ode to Hypnagogic States" in *Up the River*; "Mickies" in *General Store Poems*.

The author's acknowledgments appear in the Preface.

*For my children and grandchildren
who despite my grave concerns about these times
make me hopeful about the future.*

Contents

Preface, vii

Twilight in November, 3
Imagination, 4
My Wife, Four Months Pregnant, and I Take a Walk, 6
A Brief History of Fun, 9
Namesake: A Prologue and a Prayer, 13
Tante Chava, 15
Singer, 18
The Sense of the Question, 19
Great Blue, 21
My Mother's Salami Sandwich, 22
A Close Family, 24
Moving the Firewood , 27
Last Act, 28
In the End, 30
Where the Dead Live, 32
Homers, 33
Orphans, 35
The World to Come, 36
The God of Disappointment, 37
The Dead Linger, 38
Memories Are Made of This, 39
Matinee, 42
Mickies, 44
Blue Heron, 48
At the Pigeon Store, 50
Turkeys in Twilight, 53
An Ode to Hypnagogic States, 54
Thoughts on a Winter Walk, 56

Contents

Meeting Emily and the Twins on a Winter Walk, 57
Dick and Jane, 60
Over, 62
Heaven, 64
Storm, 65
Exactly This, 66
CD Launch , 68
Pavilion, 71
Closing, 72
Senior Wellness, 74
The Poet Needs to Know Words, 76
Words Fail Me, 78
In the Beginning, 81

About the Poet, 88

Preface

Readers familiar with my earlier publications, *Indian Summer* (2011) and *General Store Poems* (2014), will see some of the same themes continued: family and friends, the so-called real and imaginary world I inhabit, and increasingly as I age, poems about aging and death.

    I wrote these poems for you, to engage and seduce you, to draw you close so I would feel less alone. I hope that you will take a long bath in this book and emerge not cleansed, but more in touch with your own feelings, experiences and memories. In showing you some of what is inside me, I hope that you will grow closer to what is inside you.

I am in the debt of so many people who have listened to or read my poems and offered me edits and suggestions. I have also had the good fortune to be part of an engaging and encouraging poetry scene in upstate New York and western Massachusetts.

    The editor and assistant editor of this book were Susan Shepard and Bailey Shepard, who are also my daughter and granddaughter. Their knowledge and competence have improved many of the poems. In matters of grammar and punctuation I have stood corrected, often. Significant editorial assistance was provided by my publisher at Square Circle Press, Richard Vang. Beyond this assistance, his engagement and devotion to this project has been everything a writer could ask. His influence and his care is evident on every page. I have also learned much from the shared feedback of a number of poetry friends: Trina Porte, Annie Karpenstein and Evelyn Atreya.

    I have been a member of Bernadette Mayer's Poetry Seminar, also the Poesy Café Group, Sunday Four, the Second Sunday at Two, and Rootdrinker's Pine Hollow Open Mic readings for many years and benefited greatly from the experience and discussions with other group members. I'm grateful to all who have participated in these groups, particularly Alan Casline, Edie Abrams, Dennis Sullivan, Dan Wilcox and Tom Corrado. I am particularly grateful to Alan Casline, who published my *General Store Poems* in 2014. (Benevolent Bird Press, a Rootdrinker Publication).

What can I say about the experience of working with Bernadette Mayer? She has been trying to drive me crazy for years, that she hasn't yet succeeded is my loss.

There are others that I should mention but the list is long and my memory less than reliable. Be assured that I am grateful to each of you. One who will not go unmentioned is my wife, Libby, who has been at my side for the last fifty-plus years. I would not be whoever I am without her.

Howard J. Kogan
Stephentown, New York (2016)

A Chill in the Air

Twilight in November

The sky is still lit but on the ground it's night.
I search the sky and towering bare trees whistling
for the missing homers. I don't see them.
This morning when I left they were on the loft
with wings outspread to the waning autumn sun.

Returning at five-thirty I find only a clump of bloody
blue feathers lying on the grass. A hawk has attacked
and the flock has fled into the safety of the sky.
I doubt they'll return today, but reluctant to leave
I wait and whistle. Then as I turn to go I hear

the rustle of wings and see one, then another
and another fly out of the dusky sky onto the loft.
In a moment all but one young blue has returned.
I will dream this night of the rustle of wings
and angels dropping through heaven's gate.

Imagination

This poem does not have a radio playing
in the background, though if it did, it would be
Ella Fitzgerald singing *Imagination*, as only she can.

We're not at the movies but if we were, it would be
a black and white French film, so poorly subtitled that after
a few minutes we would stop trying to read them.

We'd sit in the dark watching the flickering screen
mesmerized by a woman who might be Edith Piaf,
as she talks quietly with a man who was her lover,

or he may be a brother she hasn't seen in years,
or a stranger who will become her lover.
When the movie ends, we walk up Broadway

to get a cup of coffee. Just as we step inside
the lights in the rear of the coffee shop go out;
we're told it's too late, the place is closed.

No one is there except the counterman,
but if someone were there, it would be William Powell
and Myrna Loy with a wire-haired fox terrier.

You'd say, *Look! It's Nick and Nora Charles and Asta.*
I guess we could keep walking to look for another
coffee shop but I can't understand why this place

won't stay open in my own poem.
I ask the counterman if he realizes who I am.
He tells me he doesn't care who I am; he's closing.

You tell me I should have told you we were going
to see Nick and Nora in the poem so you could
have dressed for it. Did we see them?

At the corner of Eighty-sixth two cops
are in the middle of the street to block traffic.
A brass band, the kind that plays at New Orleans funerals

rounds the corner, high-stepping, striding onto Broadway
raucously playing *When the Saints Go Marching In.*
You say, *Please! Enough is enough!* And the poem ends.

My Wife, Four Months Pregnant, and I Take a Walk

On our October walk we stop to watch
an old garter snake weave in and out
of a stone wall flowing restlessly
through a lost world, nudging aside fallen
leaves, appearing, disappearing, a snake—
then only a quiver in the leaves.

Though by some people's calculation
a lower member of our congregation,
she knows the season and seeks a winter home.
Now she stops to rest on a sunlit rock.
She lifts her head to flick a fork-tongued lick,
no doubt to you.

A tribute, I think, to what you hold
in common—the seed of future generations.
She knows you're pregnant—she can taste
it on the air—and recognizes you two hold
the future in gestation. You talk of Eden
as we're prone to do.

That fairy tale runs deep but don't insult her
with biblical accusations. She had no role
in what was lost—if anything was lost—
beyond her reputation. She was drafted
for that holy war—like that first unfortunate pair.
Her plan is ours, to survive winter

to bring new life in spring.
See how she flattens on the stone,
she's a sun worshiper like you.
She wants to carry the last of summer's heat
to her winter den; summer is the only
paradise she knows.

She knows too it will soon be lost.
Look, now she's found her home
by some remembered scent,
the hole is there beside the stone.
A final glance and she pours into it
leaving us here alone.

→

Her leaving gives me pause,

as if by leaving

she meant to tell us to end this roam

not to tarry

to turn us back to home

to remind us what we carry.

A Brief History of Fun

Of all the things to think of now
as I look back,
I don't think I had much fun.
Not that I'm from fun people.
I don't think my parents had fun.
Their parents didn't even have food.

That's why they came to America,
that's what it meant in 1910:
an end to Easter pogroms,
an end to forced conscription,
an end to near starvation.
Not that there was always food
in America, but it was better.

Here the children had a chance.
That's what America was,
a country where the children had a chance.
My grandparents had miserable lives,
my parents did a little better
from that better
my generation was launched.
We knew the language,

→

we went to school and kept going;
we had to because our parents
hadn't had the opportunity.
Education was the opportunity
in the land of opportunity.

Now we're parents and grandparents
of a generation that's having fun,
something my grandparents never heard of.
These kids know they're Americans,
nothing hyphenated about it,
no first generation insecurity,
no second generation guilt.

Still I worry.
How can you know who you are
if you don't know where you're from
and don't see where you're going?

Imagine, in a hundred years,
going from not having enough to eat
to working out in spin classes,
fussing over your BMI.
From walking out of Russia
with only the clothes they wore,
(they walked for weeks)

to riding around national parks,

thirty miles a day

on fancy touring bicycles—for fun.

What I think about is

I'm the only one who knows them.

The grandparents who walked out of Russia

and the grandchildren on their bicycles.

When I finally close my eyes,

it will be as if my grandparents

and my parents never were.

I get texts from the grandchildren's

smart phones. I can see their photos

on my phone an instant after they were taken

twenty-five hundred miles away.

In 1920, when my grandmother's sister died

in Russia, she didn't find out about it for months.

They had to ask the Rabbi whether to sit shiva.

What I wish is that all of us could meet,

grandparents, grandchildren

and everyone in between.

At first we'd feel awkward

but between stories of the old country,

showing off the smart phones,   →

and the questions of how do you say this
in Yiddish or English,
amidst the grandparents' dark heavy clothes
and the grandchildren's neon bright outfits,
the complaints about how thin the grandchildren are
and their questions about who this or that relative is,
I'd like to think there would come a moment.
A moment of recognition
and in that moment
we would all know who we are.

Namesake: A Prologue and a Prayer

My father's uncle, Jowel Iliwitzki died on the 17th of March 1940 at the Sachenhausen Concentration Camp. I was born on July 9th 1940 and, in the tradition of the Ashkenazi, named for him. When he was arrested he was 51, living in Leipzig, Germany as a successful mining engineer. He had a Polish girlfriend, Dina Riwosch, much loved by the family, as was he.

Returning to his apartment one evening, he found a summons on his door to report to the police station. A neighbor warned him not to go, to run for the border or go into hiding. But he said he'd be fine, he was an educated person, a valuable asset to the country, despite being Jewish. He was brought home a few hours later by the Gestapo. The neighbor and his wife fled that night.

Tradition holds that naming a child after a dead person keeps both their name and memory alive. For believers there is a metaphysical bond between the soul of the infant and the soul of the deceased. But neither of us is a believer. We know nothing of Dina, only that she did not survive the war. She might have been killed by the Nazis, or disease, or allied bombing.

→

One does not speak ill of the dead, certainly not ill of a beloved family member and yet Jowel was criticized for being naïve, almost for being complicit in his own death, the way a smoker might be blamed for his lung cancer. But maybe he went because he was summoned, that his inclination was to do as he was asked. It's something I'd do myself.

Dear Jowel, I don't need your name.
There's no shortage of dead Jews to be named after.
Listen to your neighbor; don't go to the police station.
Take Dina and run for the border, outsmart the Nazis
and history and live in New York City where you
and Dina could come to dinner on Sundays
and tell the story of how you were summoned
to the police station, of how you ran instead.
Come and tell the story of your escape to a wide-
eyed boy whose name we do not know, but who
asks you to tell the story over and over again
as if it were his story too.

Tante Chava

Of all who gathered on those rare occasions
I am the only one left who remembers Tante Chava.
I write this to celebrate our small relationship
and rescue her from the precarious perch
of residing in only one all too mortal mind.

I met Tante Chava no more than two or three times
at my maternal grandmother's home. I don't know
whose aunt she was, we never used *Tante* except for Chava.
It was a few years after World War II,
I was probably seven or eight.

By then I'd seen holocaust survivors with blue numbers
on their arms, numbers I was told not to stare at but were never
explained except, *It's from the camps, don't say anything.*
I didn't know what camps until I found a book
and saw photographs I've never forgotten.

She's from the time when I was learning about
but not talking about the Holocaust,
but I don't know if Tante Chava was a holocaust survivor.
I might have thought so because she was
the thinnest, oldest person I'd ever met. →

She had no English and what I remember of our meetings
is being brought to her and introduced in Yiddish
as *Esther's boy*, no name, just *Esther's boy*,
as if that was what mattered. Tante Chava would smile
and hold my hand for a long time.

She had the oldest hands I'd ever seen,
her arms were sticks,
her veins stood out like the surface roots of trees,
her lips were blue, her veins were blue,
her skin mottled with brown blotches.

I wandered among these elders gathered from another world
as they drank tea from glasses and ate bakery cookies.
I tried not to stare. Still I stared and when my eyes met
Tante Chava's across the room, she'd smile her sad smile,
wave me over with one finger and hold my hand in hers.

After those times I never saw her again, I guess she died.
I never forgot her; her name was like a musical refrain,
an incantation, if I said it she would appear with the others,
as if they were always near but needed to be summoned by name:
Sara, Yitzhak, Rifka, Moshe, Leah, Yussie, Tzvi, Chava.

There is one other memory: it's of my Aunt Rose talking about Tante Chava and saying, *She lives on tea and toast.* I don't know why but it seemed an amazing revelation. I've always remembered that about Tante Chava.
She lives on tea and toast. And in my memory and a poem.

Singer

In the nineteen-seventies when I was on the upper West side,
I ate lunch at *Famous*, a dairy restaurant on West 72nd Street,
the food was okay but I went there for the wise-cracking waiters
and to bask in the fading warmth of its Yiddish ambiance.
That's where I had lunch with Singer. Well, not exactly *with* Singer.

I used to sit at the counter and kibitz with Fieval the counterman
whose half-rolled shirt-sleeves played hide and seek
with the blue numbers on his forearm.
One day while I was deciding what to eat he motioned me close,
pointed to an old man sitting alone, and whispered:

You know who that is? (I didn't.)
It's Singer.
What's he eating?
Kasha varnishkes.
Are they good?
If they're good enough for him, they're good enough for you.

I ate the kasha varnishkes in honor of Singer and Fieval.
I still do, though now that *Famous*, Fieval and Singer are gone,
I eat them at home to recall a lost world I barely knew.

The Sense of the Question

Let me be sure I have this right:
each moment we're alive we're dying
each moment we're dying we're alive.
The only time we're not dying
is when we're already dead.
This is not a matter of semantics.
A life span is an instant against a death span.

After my father died I would smell the smoke
of White Owl cigars when no one was smoking.
I would catch sight of him walking ahead of me
on a crowded street and hurry to catch up.
I would even hear his voice.
I love the taste of his favorite meal,
calves' liver with bacon and onions.

When my mother died I had to identify
her body in the coffin before the funeral.
As I lifted the cool smooth coffin lid,
I smelled the wood of the coffin
or maybe it was her turning into a tree.
When I closed it, it slipped from my hand
and sounded like a door being slammed. →

She would've liked being a tree standing

in a high pasture shading the milk cows.

It's how I think of her now, as a shade tree.

I hear the sound of the tree in spring,

the buzz of insects, the birds singing,

I watch as the sun moves a patch of shade

around the tree as a reminder.

Great Blue

After weeks of sleepless nights—endless days
you step outside at twilight and stand thoughtless,
an abandoned house on the outskirts of town,
and watch a great blue heron slowly row by,
then one star—another and another—appears
in the darkening sky and you feel yourself rising
like a dark fish through black water
to pursue the bait of distant suns,
gaining color as you rise
and inexplicably feel happy.

My Mother's Salami Sandwich

Once when I was in the fifth grade,
I was walking home from school
and I saw my salami sandwich
lying in the gutter, though I knew
I'd eaten it for lunch.

Still it looked exactly like the salami
sandwich my mother made me.
For hours after I wondered if I'd
dropped the sandwich on the way to school.
I knew I didn't but maybe I had.

At supper that night my mother talked
about a man who'd come to the door
asking for work. She felt sorry for him.
She didn't have any work but she'd told
him to wait and made him a sandwich.

Men like that often appeared in our town,
we called them drifters or hobos.
They'd camp down in the rail yards,
wander the streets downtown,
be around a few days then disappear.

I almost told my mother about the sandwich.

I don't know why I didn't, but I'm glad I didn't.

It was bad enough I'd seen it.

I think of it now as the day I grew older,

older than my mother, and less kind.

A Close Family

We meet at Old Montefiore Cemetery
wrapping our arms around each other
whispering greetings, shivering in a chill
mercury does not register.
Thank you for coming.
Of course, of course I'd come.
We're happy to see each other but
a little hushed given the occasion.

A little later we're gathered by the grave
in a loose huddle, the Rabbi quarterbacks
us through the service. The body lowered
we take turns shoveling in the rocky soil
that thuds on the coffin like distant thunder.

Then we're back in our car,
warming our hands,
talking with each other.

We're a close family.

Close? You think we're close?

I think we're close.

We don't see each other for years.

Well I feel we're close.

I don't feel anything; I'm here because of what Yogi Berra said,
    "If you don't go to other people's funerals, they won't come to yours."

Don't you think what the Rabbi said was wonderful?

The Rabbi didn't know him.

But what he said, it was like he did.

He tripped over his name, if he didn't look at his notes he
    wouldn't know who he was burying.

It was a good turnout.

Yeah, a B+.

I didn't even know half of them.

They were probably at the wrong funeral.

Stop at the office, I have to pee. Then we'll go to the house.

Do we have to? I could skip it.

Yes, we have to. They'll have a spread, it's expected.

→

Over bagels we struggle to remember the names
of each other's children, our faces shifting
moment to moment from sunny to cloudy,
as talk drifts from graduations to divorces,
this one had a baby, that one has cancer,
this one's *cum laude*, that one's bi-polar.
Finally the conversation slows, we say our
goodbyes, lie to each other about getting
together soon and flee in our getaway car.

We're quiet on the way home as if we've
begun the journey back to our separate lives.
Or perhaps it's that we finally do feel
like a close family, and in feeling that,
realize what we've lost.

Moving the Firewood

Late summer and time to move this winter's
firewood out of the weather into the woodshed.
The garter snakes have taken to it as they do,
under every few splits I find a snake or two.
This is their favorite place, their favorite season,
I'm the trouble that comes to trouble them.
They're surprised, I'm surprised myself.
But it's mostly the same ones I keep surprising,
who keep surprising me. The sudden sunlight
sets their tongues aquiver questioning why.
How do you say in snake, *you're in the way?*
After a moment they figure it out themselves
and slide deeper into the catacomb of wood.
They won't leave Eden till the wood is gone.
In a few days they've found it and moved in.
I see them high in the woodshed peering down,
grinning at me, as I'd looked down on them.
They stay till frost calls them to their winter den,
then they all seem to leave on the same night.
In winter I find their delicate shed skins, perfect
cellophane casts, cast off, clinging to the wood.

Last Act

1. His Plea

Since it's the inevitable last act
let's do our best to get it right.
You say we don't know
who will die first and it's so
but I expect it will be me.
The actuaries are on my side.

When that time comes
please resist any temptation
to make me feel better.
Don't read the foolish cards
don't talk about the weather
or plump the pillows or busy
yourself with nonsense.

Don't talk, it's all been said,
climb into bed and hold me
the way you would a child
frightened by a summer storm
and stay until I'm gone.

2. Her Answer

If you and the actuaries are right
you don't have to worry about
any pillow plumping from me.
No last minute questions either
I know where the checkbook is
and the Will. There will be
nothing to attend to but you.

You can trust me to know how,
I don't need any instructions.
What I think about is—
Who will do it for me?
When you're gone there will
be no one who knows me,
no one to touch me.

How can you do this?
It's not right,
it's not something
you would do.

In the End

There are three questions—
Who will be there? What will be said? What will we eat?
I used to think catering from Sol Zabar's or Katz's Deli.
That's when I thought I'd have the food I no longer eat—
corned beef and pastrami sandwiches, stuffed derma,
and all those desserts—cheesecake, éclairs, cannoli.

But now I think I'd like my mother's apple cake or Aunt
Eva's sugar cookies. I haven't had either in sixty years.
I'd like my family there and my three granddaughters,
I hope they're old enough, the youngest are twelve now.
I'm not afraid of death; I'm afraid of dying.
I don't want it to be a miserable experience.

I don't want to die in my sleep; I want farewells,
a chance to thank them for the play of my life.
We can all say I love you a few more times,
but it's not something we don't say now.
I'm not religious, so it surprises me a little when
I think about final words, I think of saying Shema.

I learned it by heart as a child in the forties and never
forgot it though I've forgotten everything else.
In the thundering silence of the Holocaust's wake,
I met distantly related survivors, frail and remote,
grave as ghosts. One showed me a cross she kept
in her purse for when the Nazi's come back.

But the Shema isn't the only ending I think of,
there's Louis Armstrong doing *Stardust Memories*,
or Bernstein's recording of *Rhapsody in Blue*,
But if the girls are there I'd go with the Beatles
because they love them too, and because
they were the sound track for the best years of my life.

I think Abbey Road—we could pass around a joint,
hit the morphine paddle and go out singing the last tracks
from *Golden Slumber*s on ... *and in the end*
the love you take ... is equal to ... the love you make.
I like the idea of my granddaughters singing along
of my having one last chance at life after death.

Where the Dead Live

I have a black and white photograph taken in 1909
of my father Sol, who was four years old,
his older sister Miriam, a younger brother Joe,
his mother Leah, who looks pregnant and angry,
his father Jonah, his uncle Benny and his sister Rose.

The adults look solemn, the children frightened.
The men are in dark suits, the women in gowns,
I wouldn't be surprised if the clothes were supplied
by the photographer. Only the children seem to be
wearing their own clothes. It's a formal, posed

studio photograph taken to record a significant
moment, perhaps their arrival in the United States.
My father looks like I did at that age, as my son did
at four. I guess that means this is my family and I
wasn't kidnapped from the palace of Czar Nicholas II.

Everyone in the photo has been dead for decades. Yet,
during the long moments I visit with them, they are not
black and white images but people who are as alive as
I am. People who, as I turn away, become like fireflies
dimly sparkling in the long night at the end of our days.

Homers

On an October day the sky is doing its best
to convince us it's the right place for heaven,
even the trees are making a carnival of death
but this sky is no heaven. My homing pigeons

released yesterday are still missing save
for one old male who waits in his nest box
hour after hour cooing for his missing mate.
When I look in the loft, he questions me.

Homers are deeply tied to mate and home
and like us, forever at the mercy of loss.
Yesterday a Cooper's hawk attacked
and the flock exploded in all directions.

In the late afternoon one old male returned.
This morning when others tried to return,
two more Cooper's hawks attacked.
The sky and trees teem with migrating hawks.

→

All day the lone pigeon and I wait and worry,
I check again at five-thirty. Only the old male is there,
his voice quiet and hoarse cooing softly.
By now my sadness tells me it's about you

as much as the birds. You were the master flyer,
the reason I have pigeons, the one I stood next to
searching the skies in the long days of childhood.
The one whose loss I never mourned.

This evening I wait for you as well as the homers.
I wait against reason, against all I know and believe,
as if all that is lost is forever on the wing
trying to home through treacherous heavens.

Then, as if longing were an illuminated flight path,
all seven missing pigeons dive out of the darkening sky
and with them the old male's mate.
He is delirious, cooing and spinning in circles.

I take one last look around the compass of the sky,
the first stars have appeared, long shadows stretch east
toward another day and fade into familiar darkness.

Orphans

The dead are orphans

abandoned at the grave

who must learn the language of silence

learn the art of forgetting,

the daily practice of letting go,

the many skills of decomposition,

the slow loosening of bone from flesh,

the carving away of the remains of life.

They must learn to resist the tidal pull of memory

debriefing, honing, refining, distilling,

until they achieve perfection

at the end of days,

the nameless, the unknown, the dead.

The World to Come

(Loosely based on a Hasidic tale that tells us the world to come will be like this world—only a little different.)

1. An Elderly Man Talks to His Rabbi
So you're saying the world to come will be just like this world?
Exactly, only a little different.
What's the little difference?
A small matter, what you have now, you'll have then, the family you have here, will be the family you have there.
But the little difference?
You'll be asleep.
For a long time?
Who can tell time when they're sleeping?

2. Then He Talks to His Wife
Will there be an after?
Of course, after you'll sleep.
I'll sleep?
You'll sleep like the dead.
And you?
I'll have insomnia.

The God of Disappointment

We've had it with God and God's had it with us.
The Holocaust should have ended it. Was there truly
not one like Lot among them, not ten righteous?

Does God dare say this was for a holy purpose?

It's no wonder that for a hundred years *the people
of the book* have turned to other books, found
the possibility of joining other worlds irresistible.

Yet other Gods seem strange and no better.
Our God is family and like family, often disappoints.
The old certainties, like easy scapegoats, are gone.

Yet without God, life is a howling loneliness.
So we invite him to our celebrations, plead, curse,
and talk with him as a child talks to an unseen friend.

Until the end when we slip into the earth with words
of praise dancing in the air for the God of Disappointment
giving him one last chance in the world to come.

The Dead Linger

The last time I saw him he thought I was my father.
When I said, *No, it's Howard, your nephew,*
he smiled and winked
to let me know he was in on the joke.

Years later I still see that wink, that smile
slide across his face and I know the dead linger among us
saying what they always have,
each gesture clear, each voice vivid.

While we, reading in the same room together,
appear here in only the faintest way.
Ghostly apparitions rustling pages, taking turns
getting each other another cup of coffee.

I wonder if whoever survives of our spectral pair
will find the other more here when they're gone.
As if dying wakes us, to give one final gift of irony
to last as long as memory.

Memories Are Made of This

I remember meeting Aunt Freda,
my father's sister, at Idlewild Airport in 1947.
I was seven. I know I was seven because
my Aunt asked my father and he told her seven.

I remember seeing her plane taxi to the terminal
and men pushing a wheeled stairway to its door.
It was a two-engine DC-2, silver except for the tail,
which was painted white with a blue star.

Freda lived in Palestine then, but had been a social
worker for the Joint in Hungary trying to reunite families
after the Holocaust, even ransoming Jewish children
hidden in Catholic orphanages before the war.

I remember my father and I standing in the arrival's
building, it was very hectic and crowded, but it was
exciting and all new to me. It was late afternoon,
almost dark, when the crowd in front of us

→

evaporated and I saw a beautiful woman walking
toward us wearing a Woman's Army Corps uniform.
My father took her suitcase. They kissed and hugged.
She kissed me on both cheeks, a new experience.

There's another version of this part of the memory.
In this version she's with her husband, Bingo, a warm,
stocky man, a Belgian doctor she'd met at the Joint.
He greets me by pinching my cheeks; I didn't like it.

In both memories, soon after Freda or Freda and Bingo
met us, we see the flight crew, pilot, co-pilot,
and stewardess, who looks like Maureen O'Hara.
Both the pilot and co-pilot are tall red heads and pale.

My Aunt points and says, *Look how handsome*
they are, all the El Al pilots are Irish.
The enemy of my enemy is my friend.
Then Bingo or maybe my father says,

The Irish are the lost tribe of Israel.
I didn't know there were any lost tribes.
I didn't even know Jews had tribes,
but I liked the idea of being like Indians.

I've talked about this memory often,
I even told it to Aunt Freda who didn't seem
to remember it, but I thought that was
because she was in her late 70's by then.

The thing is, it didn't happen, not as I
remember it, it couldn't have.
Idlewild Airport didn't open until 1948,
the year after this memory, Aunt Freda

was never in the Women's Army Corps.
El Al didn't exist until 1948 and didn't
fly to the United States until the 1950's
and it never used DC-2's.

I did have an Aunt Freda, she did work
for the Joint, her husband Bingo was a cheek
pincher. My father and I did once meet her
plane at the airport, I would swear we did.

Add to this Ingrid Bergman, who looked
like my Aunt Freda, *Casablanca*, the Andrews
Sisters, and who knows what else—
memories are made of this.

Matinee

On a muggy Fourth of July in the Berkshires
we're at a matinee of *On the Town*.
The theatre lobby looks like the lounge
of a nursing home. In the audience
are dozens of people with walkers,
wheelchairs, portable oxygen tanks.
The rest of the crowd, including us,
are mostly the ambulatory elderly.
The woman next to me starts talking
the moment we sit down. She's a fit
eighty-something, talks about where
she's from, Kew Gardens.
She asks where I'm from, Long Island,
and tells me where she lives now, she's
in Beckett, I'm in Stephentown.
She's been spending summers here
in the Berkshires for twenty years,
then last year her husband died.
She stage whispers, *I'm here with
my friend*, pointing to an elderly man
who nods but says nothing.
The play begins. During intermission she
tells me she likes it, it got a wonderful

review in the *New York Times*, and she

also ushers at Tanglewood. This area she says,

Is God's country, not that I believe in God.

On the Town is a musical set in 1944

about three sailors on leave looking

for romance in New York City.

I was four in forty-four, she was a teen.

Her friend is older, he was in the war.

In fact, he was a sailor like the actors in the play.

After the play I overhear her ask him,

How did you like it?

   It's not the way I remember 1944.

It's a musical; it's to make people happy.

   I liked it, but it's not what I remember.

No one would pay to see what you remember,

you don't even remember what you remember.

He looks at me perplexed and shrugs.

I say, *I was a little kid in 1944, I don't remember it.*

He says, nodding toward the stage,

It wasn't singing and dancing, I remember that much.

Mickies

When I was a child, migrant workers traveled north
every August to pick potatoes at Ryan's farm.
After they finished, the farmer would allow kids from
the neighborhood to gather any potatoes they missed.

Dragging a burlap feed sack though the field, gleaning
for potatoes was the highpoint of my summer. I'd fill
the sack till it outweighed me and drag it home for
the praise of providing food for the family table.

But the family didn't get all my potatoes. Some I dug
early and hid at my fort in the woods to make mickies
at secret campfires with a secret friend, who was a boy
my age, the son of migrant workers.

That was being doubly bad, first for making a fire,
and then for talking to one of *them*. My family was
nice enough to call migrant workers *Negros*, but not
nice enough to let me have anything to do with them.

James was being bad too because he'd been warned
by his parents not to be talking to folks hereabouts.
Hereabouts, that's the word he used, but it sounded
different when he said it, sweet and soft.

My fort was hidden in the woods that began behind
the migrants' shacks. James came with the workers
three years in a row in August and when he did,
it didn't take long for us to find each other.

He said they went from farm to farm all summer
but the rest of the year they lived in South Carolina.
Sometimes we'd go to the pond to bean frogs, but
mostly we'd look for snakes or hide out in my fort.

The idea was to stay away from grown-ups,
which wasn't hard because nobody came in the woods,
and my fort was a secret from everybody I didn't like,
which was pretty much everybody.

→

When we met that first year, we met in the woods.
We looked at each other until one of us finally spoke.
It got easier after that except for the first time we'd meet.
We were both shy and nervous; we'd say the same

things over and over and not really look at each other.
But after a while we were okay and we talked like
a whole year hadn't passed. Aside from those days,
we never saw each other, so each time there was never

any certainty James and I would see each other again.
That's what happened after three summers.
It was the year the farmer got a big mechanical
harvester and no longer needed so many workers.

A few did come but James wasn't with them.
I never saw him or heard his voice again.
I liked the way he talked, the sound of his words
though he said it was me that talked funny.

But I didn't mean he talked funny, it's just
hard for a boy to say to another boy he likes
the sound of his voice. Even if James was talking
about his Mammy chopping a chicken's head off,

he made it sound like something gentle and kind.
I'd try to get him to talk when we were together
just to hear his voice but he was quiet like me.
Later we'd make a campfire and roast mickies.

It took a while to collect wood, we'd use dry grass
and kitchen matches I took from home to start it,
then wait till the coals got red to put the potatoes in.
We'd sit there talking or not talking, watching mickies

char and spit in the fire until they were done.
Then we'd push them out of the fire and wait until
they stopped smoking. We'd cut into the sweet heart
of the mickies and eat them with spoons from the 5&10.

Nothing tasted as good as those mickies seasoned by a secret
friendship of two bad boys alone together in the woods.

Blue Heron

On the eve of Rosh Hashanah, this pilgrim set
off walking in a small wood to look for God.
I wondered if trees could be God or the plants
and grasses covering every inch of ground,
the whole earth itself, the mute watchful clouds.
Some say yes but if everything is God,
is anything God? I'm looking for God
but if God is playing hard to get then
I won't find God—and I wouldn't be the first.
I hear the call of Canada Geese high above,
it seemed promising, the heavens would be
the right place for God. A flock of Canada
geese with their forlorn cry like a ram's horn
as melancholy as a sacred chant, could be God,
but it's autumn and they're flying north.
I think God has a better sense of direction.
As the wind rose I ruminated on its being invisible,
seen only by its effect, that may be the way of God.
I came upon a stream and followed it until I met
a great blue heron meditating in the shallows.
It spread it wings and slowly, silently rose
like a ghost and flew out of sight up the stream.
I followed. Soon I came upon the heron again,

it flew again. I tried not to take it personally.
Then as I stood there watching the heron fly
away, it turned and flew toward me.
It flew over me slowly and quietly more
like the spirit of a heron than a heron itself.

I heard a sound as it passed, as if it whispered,
or perhaps it was only the sound of its wings.
It flew out of sight. I didn't see it again,
though if I close my eyes I can still see it
and feel the faint breeze from its wings
flowing over me like a blessing.

At the Pigeon Store

The older men I knew as a boy weren't schooled
but they knew what they knew. They knew birds,
which meant pigeons because that was the only bird.
That's why I hung out with them.
They knew kids, there were two kinds,
good kids and good for nothing kids.
Neither of them knew how to work,
both thought the world owed them a living.
These were their sons; they never talked daughters,
the daughters belonged to the wives
and while wives complained about sons,
they only talked daughters with other women.
These men knew the difference between
men and women—women had two feelings:
sad which came with tears,
and angry which came with yelling—
men one feeling, angry which came with
either yelling or icy silence.
Women were nuts, men were normal
men forget things or let things pass
women, like elephants, never forget anything
and they never let men forget either.
Sometimes the men talked about their fathers

mostly coming of age stories of becoming
strong enough to knock their fathers down
when they hit their mothers, after that, the fathers
seemed to wilt and never hit any of them again.
Despite these men's toughness, roughness,
they were men who never hit their wives
and rarely hit their children.
When they did argue with their wives
it was usually about her spending money
on the sly for carpeting or furniture.
Often these fights would end with him
storming out and going to his mother's
or the pigeon store which seemed to be open
day and night, a clubhouse as much as a store.
Wherever he went he'd be told he was wrong.
His mother would tell him, *You're such a dope
just like your father*, kiss him and make him dinner
or if he ended up in the pigeon store
he'd be told, *You know you got shit for brains.
Your wife's a woman. Women want nice things.
You're making good money—don't be a tight-ass.*

→

I'd be sent for Italian or Chinese food
and by the time I got back they'd be talking
pigeons like nothing happened.

Later in life these men got softer, rounder
but they were still bulls and crazy for the birds.
Their sons, even the good for nothing ones,
mostly wore suits to work, and their daughters
were nurses or teachers and mothers themselves.
They'd return with their families every other Sunday
for the usual talk, pasta and gravy and whatever
game was on TV because if you're part of a family,
where your parents live will always be the place
you return, like pigeons coming home from a race.

Turkeys in Twilight

A normal person might worry at the way their mood
lifts when they see wild turkeys selecting gizzard stones
as they meander up the drive, but I'm used to me.
These turkey gangs of hens and young often form when
hens with poults encounter each other on their rambles.
There's safety in numbers and turkeys are deeply social
so after a day or two roaming together, they're inseparable.
Food is plentiful; East Creek is flowing and this many
hens will discourage most predators. I watch as they turn
from the drive, follow the edge of the grass as one hen
or another keeps an eye on me. The rest inspect
the ground, dart after grasshoppers, strip seeds off
weed heads and slowly drift down the hill into the woods.

Now the sun has tangled itself in the trees
and the darkening sky, like a slow-motion magician,
reveals the stars it's been hiding in plain sight.

An Ode to Hypnagogic States

At the library there was a college girl I sat
next to when I was in the sixth grade.
She had a gap in her blouse and I couldn't take my
eyes off her breast nestled inside the white, lacy bra.

She saw I was looking and caught my eye.
I blushed purple but she smiled and winked.
She's still winking. I never saw her again.
Or I saw her when I left the library

standing with a girlfriend. She pointed at me
and they laughed. I'm still standing there mortified.
Or we kept seeing each other every once in a while
at one place or another the way that can happen

until one day in my senior year in high school,
she arrived as my English teacher.
I wrote a composition about the experience
at the library and she gave me an *F*

or an *A* or she pretended not to remember me
or she remembered, but I was so shy
I pretended not to remember her.
Or the crush I had on my English teacher

had nothing to do with the girl in the library.
Or the experience with the girl in the library
never happened or many years later
after I finished college we met again.

She was married to a man I worked with
who left her a few years later and we dated.
She became my wife or she didn't.
My imagined life as real as the life I lived.

Thoughts on a Winter Walk

I'm in the woods on a January day
walking away from myself,
watching my footwork,
looking for the path of least regret.
The crows, witnesses for the prosecution,
fly from tree to tree, chastising.
These are not poetry woods, but woods as they are—
rotting trunks, twisted saplings, thorny thickets, a junkyard woods.
A good place to turn an ankle, to lose your bearings,
to surrender to the sweet anesthesia of cold and snow.
No one will trouble these woods 'til deer season.
By then the bones and rags will offer nothing
but the satisfaction of a mystery solved.
People will imagine it was a heart attack,
the news of my death will be passed like a dish
at the Fire Department's corned beef and cabbage dinner.
What business did he have in the woods at his age?
Some people don't know how to be old!
Then, as it does, the talk will turn to other things.

Meeting Emily and the Twins on a Winter Walk

Walking along our rural road
on a mild February day I meet
Emily taking a walk with her
little twin sisters dawdling behind.

She tells me she has to watch the twins
until her mother gets home from work,
lest I think a fourteen year old would
willingly take a walk with children.

I ask the twins how old they are.
They look at Emily.
She says, *They're five.*
The twins nod yes and look at me.
I say, *I'm seventy-two.*
They look at their sister.
She says, *He's as old as grandpa.*
They nod again.

→

A half hour later on my way back I meet
them standing at a small roadside cemetery.
The most prominent gravestone has
a small faded Memorial Day flag beside it.
Emily says her mother told her
they're related to the man buried there.
I know the grave—Justus Brockway,
a soldier in the Revolutionary War
who died at eighty-one in 1827.

Emily pointed at the gravestone script asking,
Can you make that out?
   The Will of God is Accomplished … so be it.
What does it mean?
   I guess that his death was the will of God
   or maybe his life was the will of God.
One of the twins says, *He's in heaven!*
I say, *People are dying to get into heaven!*
They look confused.

Then Emily smiles, *I get it.*
The twins ask, *What?*
Emily says, *Never mind, it's grown-up talk.*

A hundred paces back up the road
I'd seen a dead tree with large oblong holes
made by a pileated woodpecker.
I tell Emily, *The twins might like to see them.*
Watch for the bird too, it's the size of a crow.
They look at Emily. She says, *We'll watch for it.*

That's all there is to tell. We all went on our way
but the memory of that walk still brings a smile today.

Dick and Jane

Would Dick and Jane be just another Dick and Jane
if we hadn't met them when we were small and scared
sitting in a dark dismal schoolhouse on Nicolai Street,
abandoned by our mothers to the Wicked Witch of the East?
How we dreaded having to read about them out loud one
at a time as Miss Gulch thrust her pointer at our hearts.
A few kids in our class could have been Dick or Jane,
a few might even have had a dog like Spot.
They read easily, unlike Mark who haltingly stuttered
through the page as if walking on hot coals, or me
whose heart became a kettle drum as I waited my turn.
Yet now as Dick and Jane turn eighty-four and persevere
as young and cute as ever while the rest of us have withered
and creased, now I find myself grateful to you,
to your vanilla friend Sally and Spot too.
It took a while but we learned to read and the dread of reading
in class became the sweet pleasure of reading on our own.
Jane holding Dick's hand, throwing a ball to Spot,
talking endlessly,

Look, look Dick, see Spot run!
Look, look a car, see the car Sally?
See the car Spot? Look out Spot!
Oh no Dick! Oh no Spot! Poor Spot.

By giving us the words, you gave us the world.
Thanks Dick and Jane. Sorry Spot.

Over

As we gray and crease our conceit about having
choices and being in control can't be sustained.
Those endless sources of pride and shame,
prove as much an illusion as the you and I we conjure
when we speak like experts on the subject of ourselves.
But accepting this is never easy.

It might take that engaging thirty-something we talk
with all evening, who gets us imagining she likes us
in a way no one has in years, until she says how much
we remind her of her grandfather, that might convince us.
Or maybe it'll be the doctor who apologetically gives us
the dreaded diagnosis then shrugs embarrassed and guilty

like a seventeen-year-old who just banged into your car.
If that doesn't do it, maybe it'll be an afternoon we're
sitting with one of our grown children and see their
worried expression and the fear in their eyes and we know
the changes we've tried to dismiss are scaring them.
However we realize it's over, the day will come.

It may be when we're watching *The Wizard of Oz*
on TV and this kid from Kansas is singing
Somewhere Over the Rainbow and we tear up.
No one wants to think about dying piece by piece
like a leper, or that our few remaining choices are
being subtracted one by one, each subtraction added

until the sum is zero, but that's life. Tell the truth,
don't you tear up when you hear Judy Garland?
Don't you wish there was somewhere over the rainbow?
We'll both be awake tonight in the wee hours,
wistful and wet-eyed
humming that song.

Heaven

As I understand it being in heaven
is like working casino security,
you can see them but they can't see you.
You watch loved ones living out their lives
shop-lifting at Walmart, trying to date,
having car trouble, arguing, aging,
metastases blooming unknown
to anyone but you.
You can see it all
resting on a cloud.
This is your reward
you're in heaven.

Storm

I went to feed the chickens in the snow
and found them settled in for the night.
They cocked their heads, looked closely,
clucked softly to ask why I was out
when any with any sense had gone to roost.
I said the storm has made me restless,
but I don't know if it's that
and they don't care.

I took the path through the woods
to stay a while in the weather,
listen to the wind enchant the trees,
let the snow coat my jacket until
it seemed I belonged to the snowy woods
like any woodland animal lingering along
snow-domed stone walls, adding my impression
to the unimpressed landscape.

Exactly This

I was reading the review
of a gallery opening
wishing I'd been there
when I realized that I had.
There were Taos paintings
with streaks of Pepto-Bismol
against a cyan sky
imitating inimitable
pink and blue hues.
There were photographs of topiary
of mythological beings
mere privet and arbor vitae
engaging though hardly as much
as the living form that walked
out of the forest to where I stood
feeling I don't know what
but not believing my eyes.
Later I wanted to tell you—
you most of all, but me too
how the beast walked
through me
circled back
turned round and round

within my bone corral

before it slept

its wet muzzle

nuzzled against my

metaphorically enlarged heart

its pulse almost

synchronizing with my beat

like an echo in a slot canyon.

What can words tell you?
I could say you had to be there
you had to experience it yourself
but then that's not art
and one person's being there
is not another's.

CD Launch

I went to a CD launch party a while back
and if someone had told me about it,
I would have envied them and felt
not being invited to CD launch parties
was precisely what was wrong with my life.

But there I was at this cool event.
The lead singer kissed me,
she introduced me to the band,
then the producer and the recording engineer,
who acted like my being there was exactly
what made the launch party awesome.

No hand shake and *a nice to meet you*.
The engineer gives me a full one-armed half-hug
with a chest thump and a fist bump and a *Hey Dude*,
so it felt like I was sort of in the business too.
No one even said I was old enough to be their father.

So I'm standing there thirty feet from the band,
sipping on my green tea-banana-strawberry smoothie—
the place was so cool it didn't have a liquor license—
and I'm listening to the music wondering,
What is wrong with me?
because there I was at the CD launch and
yet ... not there.
Not that I wasn't there, I was there,
but being there wasn't like being there.

That's what I am trying to tell you
because I need some help here,
some insight to tack me toward what's real.
There was a woman there, eight feet tall,
all legs with a neck like a heron and
arms and legs blazoned with tattoos.
Yet even with the heron three feet away—
being at this way-cool CD launch
didn't feel that cool.

→

It was like an end of the season discount launch,
though still, it was something I would
have wished I'd been at if I wasn't already there.
The heron just blew me a kiss and now that I'm
taking a closer look, I think she's a he.
Well, a kiss is still a kiss …
I know you're wishing you were at a cool CD launch
instead of listening to me kvetch about nothing.

But stay with me. I'm talking about something
that could be an essential existential truth
about how when I'm here, I'm not,
which could lead a thoughtful person like you,
to ask if you're here when you're here or
if all of us really should have been here yesterday
when, from what I hear, it was really real.

Pavilion

It's an evening in July; we're standing at the water's edge
gently swaying and listening to the breeze blend the softly
percussive wavelets into the music drifting across the lake.
The Lester Lanin Orchestra is playing at the estate that hugs
the far shore, *You'd be So Easy to Love* and *Stardust*
sweeten the night air. We are preparing to meet.

An ocean away Auschwitz has opened,
300,000 British and French soldiers
have been evacuated from Dunkirk.
40,000 were left behind.
The War is going badly, Paris has fallen,
the Battle of Britain is about to begin.
I wish I could do something, but I won't arrive
until tomorrow amidst breaking waters,
unaware of airplanes starting their engines,
U-boats gathering off-shore.

I'm still enjoying the days you never went anywhere without me
though you were not someone who'd ever have a chance to hear
Lester Lanin or visit an estate except to work in the kitchen.
A *greenhorn* barely able to read—the lake, the music was
your dream—a world eagerly awaiting my arrival—was mine.

Closing

The old store had been for sale for years
but at what he thought it was worth
it drew little interest and no takers.
Now at eighty-four he needed whatever
he could get and needed to be rid
of heating the old building, the electric,
the taxes, the endless repairs.

He needed to be done sitting in the ruins
that for eighty years had been the center of town.
These days if six or seven people came in
for a newspaper or some talk that was it.
A ghost of a store in a ghost town
with few jobs and no prospects.

So when the low-ball offer came,
a third of what seemed fair, he took it.
It was closing today, his children busy
hauling away what little they had use for.
All he wanted was an old Yankee pennant,
and an autographed photo of Joe DiMaggio.

He sat in one of the old chairs in a circle
of chairs where a dwindling number of friends
once sat and talked about the past. A few of us
were with him, looking at the floor, awkward
men at a wake, full of feeling, but so dammed-up
we couldn't think of a thing to say.

He sat slowly shaking his head telling one, then another,
If I was even sixty years old, this wouldn't be happening.
Heaven knows we understood, for each of us had seen
his work, himself, eroded by the relentless silt of time.

None of us would dare to say it out loud,
but each of us knew, and knew the others knew,
that death, the fearsome figure of our earlier years,
was drawing closer now and looking more like a friend.

Senior Wellness

In our scary new world we've gone beyond
the simple metrics of pulse, blood, and breath,
mere health won't do, what's needed now is *wellness*.

The road to wellness is littered with kale, flax seeds,
keenwa—you know, quinoa—couscous, tabbouli,
steel cut oatmeal and Icelandic yogurt.

The quest for wellness requires yoga, meditation,
luminosity brain training and dragging the sack of gristle
hanging from your neck to water aerobics, and zumba.

And don't forget to remember to keep one eye
on the scale, another on balance, a third on cholesterol,
a fourth on your BMI and a fifth on blood pressure.

The goal is to keep your blood pressure as low
as your IQ. Walking, did I mention brisk walking?
It doesn't matter where, all roads lead to the catacombs.

The regiment isn't all bad, a drop of red wine is allowed,
an occasional sliver of dark chocolate, and this clinging
to the reins of life, this puritan self-discipline is the sort of thrift

that appeals to seniors—a synapse saved is a synapse earned.
Certainly there can be no certainty, only a hope pursued
in the light of chilly actuarial statistics, that if we eat well,

stay fit and lucky—we all need luck—a gentle death will find
us in our own bed running down like a wound clock, our main-
spring relaxed, its final tick-tock taken, the dread of zumba over.

Have an apple love, don't step on the snake.

The Poet Needs to Know Words

They are his pigments and his clay, his stone
and wood, the balls he juggles should be his own,
traced to their origin, toned by their history.
Ball came to us from Old High German and French,
meaning a spherical body, and then bounced
into Middle English and Icelandic.
Of course language being what it is
and people being what they are,
someone playing with their balls
noted the Latin *testiculum* also refers
to round spheres—hence the slang *balls*.

Slang, from the Scandinavian and Icelandic *sleng*,
which means *to sling*, came into Old High German
as *schlingin*, to *toss* or *twist*, which is fine
for some balls but tough on others.
Forgive me if my testimony omits part of the ritual,
to testify comes from the same Latin word *testiculum*,
which in ancient Rome came from the practice of holding
another's balls or your own as a way of attesting
to your truthfulness. You can hear the root in *attesting*.
It will not be a surprise to any woman to learn Roman
men picked this practice up from watching baboons.

Male baboons who are friends greet one another
by fondling each other's balls.
The word *baboon* itself is derived from Old French
and refers to the monkey's expression,
a grimace, which may have something to do
with seeing another baboon,
who thinks he's your best friend,
coming up the path to greet you.

Words Fail Me

I was telling this guy at the place—you know—
the place with all that stuff—the hardware place,
I needed this thing for the sink—
not the thing on the top, the thing on the bottom—
mine leaked on the potatoes.
A washer?
Not the washer, down more.
He walks me to the plumbing section and asks,
What brand is it?
I stare at the faucets.
It's not this piece.
What piece is it?
Let me have a thing and a piece of paper.
A pencil?
That's it!
I draw the picture, he stares at it and turns it upside down.
Maybe we don't have it. This looks like a hook.
Exactly! Mine leaks on the potatoes, I'm sure you have it.
He starts pulling out drawers under the faucet display.
That's everything we have.

There it is, I say, and pick up a hooked pipe.
Oh, he says, *a trap. What size do you need?*

A regular size.

This is the most common size, plastic or metal?

It's a white one.

Okay, he says, *plastic. Can I help you with something else?*

I start patting my pockets,

I can't find my list, but I need a thing for the door.

What door?

It's the one by the kitchen sink, the pull thing.

It's for a cabinet? The handle?

No, it's a button.

A knob? We have a complete stock of cabinet hardware, follow me.

In a moment we're standing in front of a wall with dozens of knobs.

Do you see the one it is?

I don't remember what it looks like.

You could pick one you like or bring in the broken one.

Can I call my wife?

He hands me his cell phone. I tell him he better dial.

What's the number?

I start patting my pockets again,

I never call myself.

I hand him a piece of paper.

→

This says a kitchen sink trap and a 1" round bronze knob.

That's my note, where did you get it?

You just gave it to me; I thought it was your phone number.

That's not a phone number.

I know, but we don't need to call, we know what we want now.

We do?

It's the 1" round bronze knob.

He points to a display of knobs,

Is it one of these?

Those are bronze? They look brown.

That's the color of bronze.

I don't like them.

Pick whatever you like.

Then he excuses himself to help someone else.

I stare at the display, pull on a likely looking knob,

but it doesn't open anything.

In the Beginning

In the beginning
seems like a good way to start a poem
it has a familiar ring, a vague profundity,
an authoritative tone.
Of course, what follows matters,
in the beginning of the third inning
lacks the gravitas of

in the beginning God created ...
which reminds me of
in the beginning was the Word,
an idea poets like.
That's John talking about God's word
becoming flesh.
It's a trick we all keep trying to learn,

but until we do, we're sentenced
to use words to try to make sense
of ourselves and this clever universe,
to keep us from feeling lonely and unknown.
It's hard to talk about words using words
but what else do we have?
Here we are at the end of the third inning,

or the third stanza,
either way it's about time someone
got up to bat or walked into the room
and noticed the white lotus blossom encircled
by slowly swimming orange and blue koi,
each koi a single brush stroke
practiced for years so it appears effortless.

Or we can stand at the edge of a high cliff
looking down into a painted canyon watching
a paint stallion galloping with his herd
along a dry creek that was once the river
that created the canyon with water, silt, and time.
A vulture riding a column of warm air eyes us
as it lifts above the rim, its head the color of meat.

Or we can watch a gazelle being chased
by an unchaste lioness with cubs to feed,
what happens next is up to you.
This is stanza six, and on the sixth day God created
us in his own image. See what you can do.
As for me, I see poetry here, truth and even beauty.
But I promised my granddaughters

no animals would be hurt in the making of this poem.
Instead I'll ask Mother Teresa to pray for them.
She's standing there in the shade
fingering her rosary beads
laughing and whispering with Princess Diana.
They're as real as the lion cubs you see
waiting quietly in the shade of an Acacia tree.

Each ... a word in a poem,
in the world we're creating together.
But this poem has little to do with flowers,
horses, lions, gazelles or Mother Teresa.
They're only metaphors for what the poem
is about or symbols or straw men or figures
of speech that glide in and out of the poem

like Olympic skaters,
who are poets themselves
inscribing their poems on the ice
while the judges wait for them
to execute the required double axel
and follow it with a spin.
Spinning faster and faster until they're a blur

→

bent on drilling themselves into the ice,
which they would do if this were a cartoon,
but it's all words, no pictures.
The pictures are yours.
You're the only one who knows
if the skater is a man or a woman,
how tall they are, the color of their hair,

or whether they landed that double axel.
Eventually the skater stops spinning,
masks her face in a practiced smile
and skates backward around the rink
gracefully acknowledging the applause of fans
who toss bouquets of red roses,
spray painted at an Asian bodega.

The skater steps off the ice
into the arms of her Russian trainer.
One look and you know she's KGB.
Or perhaps she hides her true identity
by looking KGB and she's a poet
who risked her life publishing *samizdat*
in defiance of reason and the Kremlin.

She wears a silver fox coat,
bears little outward resemblance
to Mother Teresa
though she might be the lioness
and the skater the gazelle or be the gazelle
and the apparatchik the lioness,
or it's something else entirely.

That's the problem with words,
they can deceive as easily as inform.
Truth is beauty,
but lies are always dressed to kill.
Or the poem comes from seeing a woman
wearing a lotus blossom kerchief
with a koi border,

like the one a mother wore after chemo.
So thin she could have been in a photograph
of a concentration camp, a photograph
because that's as close as the word can get to life.
Here we find our poem's true subject,
for God works in unspeakable ways,
never explaining anything

→

though it's said we're created in God's image

and ought to be able to understand

as well as children understand parents,

which is better than you think.

Or there's been some mistake

and we are only God's mirror image;

2-D not 3-D, and so we lack depth.

That's the sort of poem we're writing,

complex, even confusing,

but one that inevitably fails.

Because words can carry you only so far,

the possibilities are endless,

but in the end only one

possibility is lived.

That's why

there will always be another poem.

In the beginning

was the Word,

in the end will be a silence

that speaks with an eloquence

words can only envy.

About the Poet

Howard J. Kogan is a psychotherapist and poet. He and his wife, Libby, live in the Taconic Mountains in rural Upstate New York. His poems have appeared in *Still Crazy*, *Occu-poetry*, *Poetry Ark*, *Naugatuck River Review*, *Jewish Currents Anthology*, *Literary Gazette*, *Pathways*, *Up the River*, *Point Mass Anthology*, *Misfit Magazine*, *Flair*, and *Award Winning Poems from Smith's Tavern Poet Laureate Contest* (2010 and 2011 Editions). His 2011 book of poems, *Indian Summer*, is available from Square Circle Press. His chapbook, *General Store Poems*, published by Benevolent Bird Press in 2014, is available from the author.

About his writing he says, "After setting aside writing poetry in my twenties to attend to family and career, I returned to it in my sixties. I'm grateful to have this opportunity to return to an early love and give voice to the inner thoughts, perceptions, and memories that have been my constant and (mostly) welcome companions."

Also Available From Square Circle Press

Indian Summer
poems by Howard J. Kogan

Howard J. Kogan began writing poetry in his twenties, but set it aside to pursue family life and a career as a social worker and psychotherapist. In his sixties he returned to writing poetry, a time he wistfully refers to as his "Indian summer." In 2011, Howard was named Poet Laureate of Smith's Tavern, an annual contest held in Voorheesville featuring the top poets of New York's Capital Region. This first collection of fifty poems includes the six he submitted for the 2010 and 2011 Smith's Tavern contests.

ISBN: 978-0-9833897-3-6
124 pages, softcover
$12.95

www.SquareCirclePress.com

www.ingramcontent.com/pod-product-compliance
Lightning Source LLC
Chambersburg PA
CBHW051659040426
42446CB00009B/1213